CW00550202

Best Air Fryer Cookbook 2021

Easy Home-Made and Must-Try Delicious Recipes for Food and Meat Lovers!

Martine Haley

Table of Contents

—

INTRODUCTION

An air fryer is a kitchen appliance designed to deliver a tasty, crispy, golden-brown morsel of food without the use of oil or other cooking fats. It uses hot air instead of oil or other cooking fats to cook food quickly and evenly.

The air fryer can be used for making fried chips in addition to other foods.

There are several varieties of air fryers. One of the main categories is made up of countertop air fryers designed for individual use in the kitchen. These models sit on the worktop or counter top and feature a basket that sits on a wire rack. This forms the base that holds hot air that cooks food as it passes through it.

air fryer's air fryers are designed to help you make healthy and filling meals. Our electric fryers are perfect for people who want fresh, homemade fries without all of the fat. Our air fryer features a lightweight aluminum design that lets you move the appliance from room to room without worry. Each air fryer is also equipped with a thermostat, making it easy to adjust the temperature as needed.

An air fryer is an appliance that cooks food using high-speed air circulation. It is a perfect alternative to deep frying, baking or roasting, and works great for cooking fast and healthy meals.

How Does an Air Fryer Work?

The fan draws warm air from the bottom of the chamber, which rises and cools as it circulates. The food is then placed in the middle of the basket, and the fan circulates air around it, cooking it all at once. Food cooks faster than if you fried it in oil or baked it in an oven. The food doesn't become soggy like fried food does, either. Because the air circulates around the food rather than through it, you can use much less oil in your Air Fryer. Best of all, since no oil is being used for cooking, there's much less of an environmental impact!

What Types of Air Fryers are Available?

Air fryers come in a variety of sizes as well as different colors and designs. You may find one that has a View Master-like chrome trim or one with a retro design pattern that blends easily into your décor. Some Air fryers are as small as a rice cooker while others can be used to make large batches of French fries with recipes you create on your tablet! Some Air Fryer models have "smart" features that allow you to cook multiple foods at the same time; others have timers so you can automatically set them for particular times during the day. All versions sterilize their own cooking plates by running them through a clean cycle between batches!

When you are looking for a new air fryer, you should take a look at air fryer Cookware. We have all of the features you are looking for in an air fryer, including built in racks that will allow you to cook a full size meal for your family. We also have a variety of accessories that will give you an even better cooking experience.

We are proud to introduce air fryer Cookware, the premier brand in air fryers. You can rest assured that we only use the best materials to ensure our products will work for years to come. Our air fryers feature built-in racks, so you can cook a full-size meal at once. They also include an adjustable thermostat that ranges from 120 to 500 degrees Fahrenheit.

Whether you are looking to impress your family with gourmet French fries or just want to make your favorite chicken drumsticks and vegetables, air fryer Cookware has everything you need. Every item has been carefully tested to ensure safe and responsible use. All of our products carry a One Year Limited Manufacturer Warranty, so you can be confident that they will serve your needs well.

Lemony Drumsticks

Preparation Time: 5 minutes

Cooking Time: 20 minutes

Servings: 2

Ingredients:

- Baking powder – 2 tsps.
- Garlic powder – ½ tsp.
- Chicken drumsticks – 8
- Salted butter – 4 tbsps. melted
- Lemon pepper seasoning – 1 tbsp.

Directions:

1. Sprinkle garlic powder and baking powder over drumsticks and rub into chicken skin. Place drumsticks into the air fryer basket. Cook at 375F for 25 minutes. Flip the drumsticks once halfway through the Cooking Time.

2. Remove when cooked. Mix seasoning and butter in a bowl. Add drumsticks to the bowl and toss to coat. Serve.

Nutrition: Calories 532; Carbs 1.2g; Fat 32.3g; Protein 48.3g

Parmesan Chicken Tenders

Preparation Time: 5 minutes

Cooking Time: 10 minutes

Servings: 4

Ingredients:

- 1 pound chicken tenderloins
- 3 large egg whites
- ½ cup Italian-style bread crumbs
- ¼ cup grated Parmesan cheese

Directions:

1. Preparing the Ingredients. Spray the Cuisinart air fryer basket with olive oil. Trim off any white fat from the chicken tenders. In a bowl, whisk the egg whites until frothy. In a separate small mixing bowl, combine the bread crumbs and Parmesan cheese. Mix well.

2. Dip the chicken tenders into the egg mixture, then into the Parmesan and bread crumbs. Shake off any excess breading. Place the

chicken tenders in the greased Cuisinart air fryer basket in a single layer. Generously spray the chicken with olive oil to avoid powdery, uncooked breading.

3. Air Frying. Set the temperature of your Cuisinart AF to 370°F. Set the timer and bake for 4 minutes. Using tongs, flip the chicken tenders and bake for 4 minutes more. Check that the chicken has reached an internal temperature of 165°F. Add Cooking Time if needed. Once the chicken is fully cooked, plate, serve, and enjoy.

Nutrition: Calories: 210; Fat: 4g; Saturated fat: 1g; Carbohydrate: 10g; Fiber: 1g; Sugar: 1g; Protein: 33g;

Easy Lemon Chicken Thighs

Preparation Time: 5 minutes

Cooking Time: 10 minutes

Servings: 4

Ingredients:

- Salt and black pepper to taste
- 2 tablespoons olive oil
- 2 tablespoons Italian seasoning
- 2 tablespoons freshly squeezed lemon juice
- 1 lemon, sliced

Directions:

1. Place the chicken thighs in a medium mixing bowl and season them with the salt and pepper. Add the olive oil, Italian seasoning, and lemon juice and toss until the chicken thighs are thoroughly coated with oil. Add the sliced lemons. Place the chicken thighs into the air fryer basket in a single layer.

2. Set the temperature of your AF to 350°F. Set the timer and cook for 10 minutes. Using

tongs, flip the chicken. Reset the timer and cook for 10 minutes more. Check that the chicken has reached an internal temperature of 165°F. Add Cooking Time if needed. Once the chicken is fully cooked, plate, serve, and enjoy.

Nutrition: Calories 325Carbs 1g; Fat 26g; Protein 20g

Air Fryer Grilled Chicken Breasts

Preparation Time: 5 minutes

Cooking Time: 14 minutes

Servings: 4

Ingredients

- ½ teaspoon garlic powder
- salt and black pepper to taste
- 1 teaspoon dried parsley
- 2 tablespoons olive oil, divided
- 3 boneless, skinless chicken breasts

Directions:

1. Preparing the Ingredients. In a small bowl, combine together the garlic powder, salt, pepper, and parsley. Using 1 tablespoon of olive oil and half of the seasoning mix, rub each chicken breast with oil and seasonings. Place the chicken breast in the air fryer basket.

2. Air Frying. Set the temperature of your Cuisinart AF to 370°F. Set the timer and grill for 7 minutes.

3. Using tongs, flip the chicken and brush the remaining olive oil and spices onto the chicken. Reset the timer and grill for 7 minutes more. Check that the chicken has reached an internal temperature of 165°F. Add Cooking Time if needed.

4. When the chicken is cooked, transfer it to a platter and serve.

Nutrition: Calories 182Carbs 0g; Fat 9g; Protein 26g

Crispy Air Fryer Butter Chicken

Preparation Time: 5 minutes

Cooking Time: 15 minutes

Servings: 4

Ingredients:

- 2 (8-ounce) boneless, skinless chicken breasts
- 1 sleeve Ritz crackers
- 4 tablespoons (½ stick) cold unsalted butter, cut into 1-tablespoon slices

Directions:

1. Preparing the Ingredients. Spray the Cuisinart air fryer basket with olive oil, or spray an air fryer–size baking sheet with olive oil or cooking spray.

2. Dip the chicken breasts in water. Put the crackers in a resealable plastic bag. Using a mallet or your hands, crush the crackers. Place the chicken breasts inside the bag one

at a time and coat them with the cracker crumbs.

3. Place the chicken in the greased air fryer basket, or on the greased baking sheet set into the air fryer basket. Put 1 to 2 dabs of butter onto each piece of chicken.

4. Air Frying. Set the temperature of your Cuisinart AF to 370°F. Set the timer and bake for 7 minutes.

5. Using tongs, flip the chicken. Spray the chicken generously with olive oil to avoid uncooked breading. Reset the timer and bake for 7 minutes more.

6. Check that the chicken has reached an internal temperature of 165°F. Add Cooking Time if needed. Using tongs, remove the chicken from the air fryer and serve.

Nutrition: Calories: 750; Fat: 40g; Carbohydrate: 38g; Protein: 57g;

Light and Airy Breaded Chicken Breasts

Preparation Time: 5 minutes

Cooking Time: 15 minutes

Servings: 2

Ingredients:

- 2 large eggs
- 1cup bread crumbs or panko bread crumbs
- 1 teaspoon Italian seasoning
- 4 to 5 tablespoons vegetable oil
- 2 boneless, skinless, chicken breasts

Directions:

1. Preparing the Ingredients. Preheat the Cuisinart air fryer to 370°F. Spray the Cuisinart air fryer basket with olive oil or cooking spray. In a small bowl, whisk the eggs until frothy. In a separate small mixing bowl, mix together the bread crumbs, Italian seasoning, and oil. Dip the chicken in the egg mixture, then in the bread crumb mixture.

Place the chicken directly into the greased air fryer basket, or on the greased baking sheet set into the basket.

2. Air Frying. Spray the chicken generously and thoroughly with olive oil to avoid powdery, uncooked breading. Set the timer and fry for 7 minutes. Using tongs, flip the chicken and generously spray it with olive oil. Reset the timer and fry for 7 minutes more. Check that the chicken has reached an internal temperature of 165°F. Add Cooking Time if needed. Once the chicken is fully cooked, use tongs to remove it from the air fryer and serve.

Nutrition: Calories: 833; Fat: 46g; Carbohydrate: 40g; Protein: 65g;

Chicken Fillets, Brie & Ham

Preparation Time: 5 minutes

Cooking Time: 15 minutes

Servings: 4

Ingredients:

- 2 Large Chicken Fillets
- Freshly Ground Black Pepper
- 4 Small Slices of Brie (Or your cheese of choice)
- 1 Tbsp Freshly Chopped Chives
- 4 Slices Cured Ham

Directions:

1. Preparing the Ingredients. Slice the fillets into four and make incisions as you would for a hamburger bun. Leave a little "hinge" uncut at the back. Season the inside and pop some brie and chives in there. Close them, and wrap them each in a slice of ham. Brush with oil and pop them into the basket.

2. Air Frying. Heat your fryer to 350° F. Roast the little parcels until they look tasty (15 min)

Nutrition: Calories: 850 Carbs: 43 g Fat: 50 g Protein: 76 g

Air Fryer Cornish Hen

Preparation Time: 5 minutes

Cooking Time: 30 minutes

Servings: 2

Ingredients:

- 2 tablespoons Montreal chicken seasoning
- 1 (1½- to 2-pound) Cornish hen

Directions:

1. Preheat the Cuisinart air fryer to 390°F. Rub the seasoning over the chicken, coating it thoroughly.

2. Put the chicken in the basket. Set the timer and roast for 15 minutes.

3. Flip the chicken and cook for another 15 minutes. Check that the chicken has reached an internal temperature of 165°F. Add Cooking Time if needed.

Nutrition: Calories: 520; Fat: 36g; Carbohydrate: 0g; Protein: 45g;

Air Fried Turkey Wings

Preparation Time: 5 minutes

Cooking Time: 26 minutes

Servings: 4

Ingredients:

- 2 pounds turkey wings
- 3 tablespoons olive oil or sesame oil
- 3 to 4 tablespoons chicken rub

Directions:

1. Put the turkey wings in a large mixing bowl. Pour the olive oil into the bowl and add the rub. Using your hands, rub the oil mixture over the turkey wings. Place the turkey wings in the air fryer basket.

2. Fix the temperature of your Air Fryer to 380°F. Set the timer and roast for 13 minutes.

3. Using tongs, flip the wings. Reset the timer and roast for 13 minutes more. Remove the

turkey wings from the air fryer, plate, and serve.

Nutrition: Calories: 521; Fat: 34g; Carbohydrate: 4g; Protein: 52g;

Chicken-Fried Steak Supreme

Preparation Time: 10 minutes

Cooking Time: 30 minutes

Servings: 8

Ingredients:

- ½ pound beef-bottom round, sliced into strips
- 1 cup of breadcrumbs
- 2 medium-sized eggs
- Pinch of salt and pepper
- ½ tablespoon of ground thyme

Directions:

1. Preparing the Ingredients. Cover the basket of the Air fryer with a layer of tin foil, leaving the edges open to allow air to flow through the basket. Preheat the air fryer to 350 degrees. In a bowl, whisk the eggs until fluffy and until the yolks and whites are fully combined, and set aside. In a separate bowl, mix the breadcrumbs, thyme, salt and pepper, and set aside. One by one, dip each

piece of raw steak into the bowl with dry ingredients, coating all sides; then submerge into the bowl with wet ingredients, then dip again into the dry ingredients. This double coating will ensure an extra crisp air fry. Lay the coated steak pieces on the foil covering the air-fryer basket, in a single flat layer.

2. Air Frying. Set the Cuisinart air fryer timer for 15 minutes. After 15 minutes, the air fryer will turn off and the steak should be mid-way cooked and the breaded coating starting to brown. Using tongs, turn each piece of steak over to ensure a full all-over fry. Reset the air fryer to 320 ° for 15 minutes. After 15 minutes, when the air fryer shuts off, remove the fried steak strips using tongs and set on a serving plate. Eat once cool enough to handle and enjoy.

Nutrition: Calories: 421Fat: 26gCarbs: 8gProtein: 46g

Cheesy Chicken Tenders

Preparation Time: 10 minutes

Cooking Time: 30 minutes

Servings: 4

Ingredients:

- 1 large white meat chicken breast

- 1 cup of breadcrumbs

- 2 medium-sized eggs

- Pinch of salt and pepper

- 1 tablespoon of grated or powdered parmesan cheese

Directions:

1. Cover the basket of the Air fryer with a layer of tin foil, leaving the edges open to allow air to flow through the basket. Preheat the Cuisinart air fryer to 350 degrees. In a bowl, whisk the eggs until fluffy and until the yolks and whites are fully combined, and set aside. In a separate bowl, mixt he breadcrumbs, parmesan, salt and pepper, and set aside.

One by one, dip each piece of raw chicken into the bowl with dry ingredients, coating all sides; then submerge into the bowl with wet ingredients, then dip again into the dry ingredients. Put the coated chicken pieces on the foil covering the Air fryer basket, in a single flat layer.

2. Set the Cuisinart air fryer timer for 15 minutes. After 15 minutes, the air fryer will turn off and the chicken should be mid-way cooked and the breaded coating starting to brown. Flip each piece of chicken over to ensure a full all over fry. Reset the Cuisinart air fryer to 320 degrees for another 15 minutes. After 15 minutes, when the air fryer shuts off, remove the fried chicken strips using tongs and set on a serving plate. Eat once cool enough to handle, and enjoy.

Nutrition: Calories: 278; Fat: 15g; Protein:29g;Sugar:7g

Minty Chicken-Fried Pork Chops

Preparation Time: 10 minutes

Cooking Time: 30 minutes

Servings: 4

Ingredients:

- 4medium-sized pork chops
- 1 cup of breadcrumbs
- 2 medium-sized eggs
- Pinch of salt and pepper
- ½ tablespoon of mint, either dried and ground; or fresh, rinsed, and finely chopped

Directions:

1. Preparing the Ingredients. Cover the basket of the Air fryer with a layer of tin foil, leaving the edges open to allow air to flow through the basket. Preheat the Cuisinart air fryer to 350 degrees. In a mixing bowl, whisk the eggs until fluffy and until the yolks and whites are fully combined, and set aside. In a separate bowl, mix the breadcrumbs, mint,

salt and pepper, and set aside. One by one, dip each raw pork chop into the bowl with dry ingredients, coating all sides; then submerge into the bowl with wet ingredients, then dip again into the dry ingredients. Lay the coated pork chops on the foil covering the Air fryer basket, in a single flat layer.

2. Air Frying. Set the Cuisinart air fryer timer for 15 minutes. After 15 minutes, the Air fryer will turn off and the pork should be mid-way cooked and the breaded coating starting to brown. Using tongs, turn each piece of steak over to ensure a full all-over fry. Reset the Cuisinart air fryer to 320 degrees for 15 minutes. After 15 minutes remove the fried pork chops using tongs and set on a serving plate.

Nutrition: Calories: 262Fat: 17gCarbs: 7gProtein: 32g

Bacon Lovers' Stuffed Chicken

Preparation Time: 10 minutes

Cooking Time: 20 minutes

Servings: 4

Ingredients:

- 4 (5-ounce) boneless, skinless chicken breasts, sliced into ¼ inch thick
- 2 packages Boursin cheese
- 8 slices thin-cut bacon or beef bacon
- Sprig of fresh cilantro, for garnish

Directions:

1. Preparing the Ingredients. Spray the Cuisinart air fryer basket with avocado oil. Preheat the Cuisinart air fryer to 400°F. Put one of the chicken breasts on a cutting board. With a sharp knife held parallel to the cutting board, make a 1-inch-wide incision at the top of the breast. Carefully cut into the breast to form a large pocket, leaving a ½-inch border along the sides and bottom. Repeat with the

other 3 chicken breasts. Snip the corner of a large resealable plastic bag to form a ¾-inch hole. Place the Boursin cheese in the bag and pipe the cheese into the pockets in the chicken breasts, dividing the cheese evenly among them. Wrap 2 slices of bacon around each chicken breast and secure the ends with toothpicks.

2. Air Frying. Place the bacon-wrapped chicken in the Cuisinart air fryer basket and cook until the bacon is crisp and the chicken's internal temperature reaches 165°F, about 18 to 20 minutes, flipping after 10 minutes. Garnish with a sprig of cilantro before serving, if desired.

Nutrition: Calories: 446 Fat: 17g Carbs: 13g Protein: 36g

Air Fryer Turkey Breast

Preparation Time: 5 minutes

Cooking Time: 60 minutes

Servings: 6

Ingredients:

- Pepper and salt
- 1 oven-ready turkey breast
- Turkey seasonings of choice

Directions:

1. Preheat the Cuisinart air fryer to 350 degrees.
2. Season turkey with pepper, salt, and other desired seasonings.
3. Place turkey in air fryer basket.
4. Set temperature to 350°F, and set time to 60 minutes. Cook 60 minutes. The meat should be at 165 degrees when done. Allow to rest 10-15 minutes before slicing. Enjoy.

Nutrition: Calories: 212; Fat: 12g; Protein:24g; Sugar:0g

Mustard Chicken Tenders

Preparation Time: 5 minutes

Cooking Time: 20 minutes

Servings: 4

Ingredients:

- ½ C. coconut flour
- 1 tbsp. spicy brown mustard
- 2 beaten eggs
- 1 pound of chicken tenders

Directions:

1. Season tenders with pepper and salt.
2. Place a thin layer of mustard onto tenders and then dredge in flour and dip in egg.
3. Add to the Air fryer, set temperature to 390°F, and set time to 20 minutes.

Nutrition: Calories: 346Fat: 10g Carbs: 12g Protein: 31g

Homemade Breaded Nugget In Doritos

Preparation Time: 10 minutes

Cooking Time: 15 minutes

Servings: 4

Ingredients:

- ½ lb. boneless, skinless chicken breast
- ¼ lb. Doritos snack
- 1 cup of wheat flour
- 1 egg
- Salt, garlic and black pepper to taste.

Directions:

1. Cut the chicken breast in the width direction, 1 to 1.5 cm thick, so that it is already shaped like pips.
2. Season with salt, garlic, black pepper to taste and some other seasonings if desired.
3. You can also season with those seasonings or powdered onion soup.

4. Put the Doritos snack in a food processor or blender and beat until everything is crumbled, but don't beat too much, you don't want flour.

5. Now bread, passing the pieces of chicken breast first in the wheat flour, then in the beaten eggs and finally in the Doritos, without leaving the excess flour, eggs or Doritos.

6. Place the seeds in the Air Fryer basket and program for 15 minutes at 400ºF, and half the time they brown evenly.

Nutrition: Calories: 42 Carbohydrates: 1.65g Fat: 1.44g Protein: 5.29g Sugar: 0.1g Cholesterol: 20mg

Breaded Chicken without Flour

Preparation Time: 10 minutes

Cooking Time: 15 minutes

Servings: 6

Ingredients:

- 1 1/6 oz. of grated parmesan cheese

- 1 unit of egg

- 1 lb of chicken (breast)

- Salt and black pepper to taste

Directions:

1. Cut the chicken breast into 6 fillets and season with a little salt and pepper.

2. Beat the egg in a bowl.

3. Pass the chicken breast in the egg and then in the grated cheese, sprinkling the fillets.

4. Non-stick and put in the air fryer at 4000F for about 30 minutes or until golden brown.

Nutrition: Calories: 114 Carbohydrates: 13g Fat: 5.9g Protein: 2.3g Sugar: 3.2g Cholesterol: 19mg

Barbecue with Chorizo and Chicken

Preparation Time: 5 minutes

Cooking Time: 35 minutes

Servings: 4

Ingredients:

- 4 chicken thighs
- 2 Tuscan sausages
- 4 small onions

Directions:

1. Preheat the fryer to 400°F for 5 minutes. Season the meat the same way you would if you were going to use the barbecue.
2. Put in the fryer, lower the temperature to 160°C and set for 30 minutes.
3. After 20 minutes, check if any of the meat has reached the point of your preference. If so, take whichever is ready and return to the fryer with the others for another 10 minutes,

now at 400°F. If not, return them to Air Fryer for the last 10 minutes at 400°F.

Nutrition: Calories: 135 Carbohydrates: 0g Fat: 5g Protein: 6g Sugar: 0g Cholesterol: 300mg

Roasted Thigh

Preparation Time: 5 minutes

Cooking Time: 30 minutes

Servings: 1

Ingredients:

- 3 chicken thighs and thighs
- 2 red seasonal bags
- 1 clove garlic
- ½ tsp of salt
- 1 pinch of black pepper

Directions:

1. Season chicken with red season, minced garlic, salt, and pepper. Leave to act for 5-10 minutes to obtain the flavor.
2. Put the chicken in the basket of the air fryer and bake at 390ºF for 20 minutes.
3. After that time, remove the Air Fryer basket and check the chicken spot. If it is still raw or not golden enough, turn it over and leave it for another 10 minutes at 350ºF.

4. After the previous step, your chicken will be ready on the Air Fryer! Serve with doré potatoes and leaf salad.

Nutrition: Calories: 278 Carbohydrates: 0.1g Fat: 18g Protein: 31g Sugar: 0g Cholesterol: 166mg

Coxinha Fit

Preparation Time: 10 minutes

Cooking Time: 10-15 minutes

Servings: 4

Ingredients:

- ½ lb. seasoned and minced chicken
- 1 cup light cottage cheese
- 1 egg
- Condiments to taste
- Flaxseed or oatmeal

Directions:

1. In a bowl, mix all of the ingredients together except flour.
2. Knead well with your hands and mold into coxinha format.
3. If you prefer you can fill it, add chicken or cheese.
4. Repeat the process until all the dough is gone.
5. Pass the drumsticks in the flour and put them in the fryer.

6. Bake for 10 to 15 minutes at 390°F or until golden. Now it only works!

Nutrition: Calories: 220 Carbohydrates: 40g Fat: 18g Protein: 100g Sugar: 5g Cholesterol: 3000mg

Rolled Turkey Breast

Preparation Time: 5 minutes

Cooking Time: 10 minutes

Servings: 4

Ingredients:

- 1 box of cherry tomatoes
- ¼ lb. turkey blanket

Directions:

1. Wrap the turkey and blanket in the tomatoes, close with the help of toothpicks.
2. Take to Air Fryer for 10 minutes at 3900F.
3. You can increase the filling with ricotta and other preferred light ingredients.

Nutrition: Calories: 172 Carbohydrates: 3g Fat: 2g Protein: 34g Sugar: 1g Cholesterol: 300mg

Chicken in Beer

Preparation Time: 5 minutes

Cooking Time: 10 minutes

Servings: 4

Ingredients:

- 2 ¼ lbs chicken thigh and thigh
- ½ can of beer
- 4 cloves of garlic
- 1 large onion
- Pepper and salt to taste

Directions:

1. Wash the chicken pieces and, if desired, remove the skin to be healthier.
2. Place on an ovenproof plate.
3. In the blender, beat the other ingredients: beer, onion, garlic, and add salt and pepper, all together.
4. Cover the chicken with this mixture; it has to stay like swimming in the beer.

5. Take to the preheated air fryer at 3900F for 45 minutes.

6. It will roast when it has a brown cone on top and the beer has dried a bit.

Nutrition: Calories: 674 Carbohydrates: 5.47g Fat: 41.94g Protein: 61.94g Sugar: 1.62g Cholesterol: 206mg

Chicken Fillet

Preparation Time: 5 minutes

Cooking Time: 20 minutes

Servings: 4

Ingredients:

- 4 chicken fillets
- salt to taste
- 1 garlic clove, crushed
- thyme to taste
- black pepper to taste

Directions:

1. Add seasoning to fillets, wrapping well for flavor. Heat up the Air Fryer for 5 minutes at 350°F. Place the fillets in the basket, program for 20 minutes at 350°F.
2. With 5 minutes remaining, turn the fillets and raise the temperature to 3900F. Serve

Nutrition: Calories: 90 Carbohydrates:1g Fat: 1g Protein: 17g Sugar: 0g Cholesterol: 45mg

Chicken with Lemon and Bahian Seasoning

Preparation Time: 2 hours

Cooking Time: 20 minutes

Servings: 4

Ingredients:

- 5 pieces of chicken to bird;
- 2 garlic cloves, crushed;
- 4 tablespoons of lemon juice;
- 1 coffee spoon of Bahian spices;
- salt and black pepper to taste.

Directions:

1. Place the chicken pieces in a covered bowl and add the spices. Add the lemon juice. Cover the container and let the chicken marinate for 2 hours.
2. Place each piece of chicken in the basket of the air fryer, without overlapping the pieces. Set the fryer for 20 minutes at 390ºF. In half the time, brown evenly. Serve!

Nutrition: Calories: 316.2 Carbohydrates: 4.9g
Fat: 15.3g Protein: 32.8g Sugar: 0g

Chicken Meatballs

Preparation Time: 5 minutes

Cooking Time: 15 minutes

Servings: 2

Ingredients:

- ½ lb. chicken breast
- 1 tbsp of garlic
- 1 tbsp of onion
- ½ chicken broth
- 1 tbsp of oatmeal, whole wheat flour or of your choice
- 1 pinch of paprika
- Salt and black pepper

Directions:

1. Place all of the ingredients in a food processor and beat well until well mixed and ground.
2. If you don't have a food processor, ask the butcher to grind it and then add the other ingredients, mixing well.

3. Make balls and place them in the Air Fryer basket.

4. Program the Air Fryer for 15 minutes at 400ºF.

5. Half the time shake the basket so that the meatballs loosen and fry evenly.

Nutrition: Calories: 45 Carbohydrates: 1.94g Fat: 1.57g Protein: 5.43g Sugar: 0.41g Cholesterol: 23m

Basic BBQ Chicken

Preparation Time: 5 minutes

Cooking Time: 20 minutes

Servings: 4

Ingredients:

- 2 tablespoons Worcestershire Sauce
- 1 tablespoon honey
- ¾ cup ketchup
- 2 teaspoons chipotle chili powder
- 6 chicken drumsticks

Directions:

1. Heat up the air fryer to 370 degrees F for 5 minutes.
2. Use a big bowl to mix the Worcestershire sauce, honey, ketchup and chili powder. Whisk it up well.
3. Drop in the drumsticks and turn them so they are all coated with the mixture.

4. Grease the basket of the air fryer with nonstick spray and place 3 chicken drumsticks in.

5. Cook for 17 minutes for large drumsticks 15 minutes for smaller ones, flipping when it reaches half the time.

6. Repeat with the other three drumsticks.

Nutrition: Calories: 145 Carbohydrates: 4.5g Fat: 2.6g Protein: 13g

Basic No Frills Turkey Breast

Preparation Time: 5 minutes

Cooking Time: 50 minutes

Servings: 4

Ingredients:

- 1 bone in turkey breast (about 8 pounds)
- 2 tablespoons olive oil
- 2 tablespoons sea salt
- 1 tablespoon black pepper

Directions:

1. Warm up the air fryer to 360°F for about 8 minutes.
2. Rub the washed turkey breast with the olive oil both on the skin and on the inside of the cavity.
3. Sprinkle on the sea salt and black pepper.
4. Remove the basket from the air fryer and spray with butter or olive oil flavored nonstick spray.
5. Put the turkey in with the breast side down.

6. Cook 20 minutes and carefully turn the breast over.

7. Spray with cooking oil and cook another 20 minutes.

8. When done test with thermometer and it should read 165 degrees F. If not, put it back in for a few minutes.

9. Let the breast rest at least 15 minutes before cutting and serving.

Nutrition: Calories: 375 Carbohydrates: 8.2g Fat: 6.8g Protein: 15g

Faire-Worthy Turkey Legs

Preparation Time: 5 minutes

Cooking Time: 10 minutes

Servings: 4

Ingredients:

- I turkey leg
- 1 teaspoon olive oil
- 1 teaspoon poultry seasoning
- 1 teaspoon garlic powder
- salt and black pepper to taste

Directions:

1. Warm up the air fryer to 350°F for about 4 minutes.
2. Coat the leg with the olive oil. Just use your hands and rub it in.
3. In a small bowl, mix the poultry seasoning, garlic powder, salt and pepper. Rub it on the turkey leg.
4. Coat the inside of the air fryer basket with nonstick spray and place the turkey leg in.

5. Cook for 27 minutes, turning at 14 minutes. Be sure the leg is done by inserting a meat thermometer in the fleshy part of the leg and it should read 165 degrees F.

Nutrition: Calories: 325 Carbohydrates: 8.3g Fat: 10g Protein: 18g

Herb Air Fried Chicken Thighs

Preparation Time: 5 minutes

Cooking Time: 50 minutes

Servings: 4

Ingredients:

- 2 pounds deboned chicken thighs
- 1 teaspoon rosemary
- 1 teaspoon thyme
- 1 teaspoon garlic powder
- 1 large lemon

Directions:

1. Trim fat from thighs and salt and pepper all sides.
2. In a bowl, combine the rosemary, thyme, and garlic powder. Sprinkle over the chicken thighs and press the mixture in putting them on a baking sheet.
3. Cut the lemon and squeeze the juice over all the chicken thighs. Cover with plastic wrap and put in the refrigerator for 30 minutes.

4. Warm up the air fryer to 360 degrees F for 6 minutes and spray with butter flavored cooking spray.

5. Place the thighs in the air fryer basket, as many will fit in one layer.

6. Cook for 15 minutes, turning after 7 minutes. Check internal temperature to make sure it is at 180 degrees F before serving.

Nutrition: Calories 534 Fat 27.8 g Carbohydrates 2.5 g Sugar 0.5 g Protein 66.2 g Cholesterol 202 mg

Salt and Pepper Wings

Preparation Time: 5 minutes

Cooking Time: 10 minutes

Servings: 4

Ingredients:

- 2 teaspoons salt
- 2 teaspoons fresh ground pepper
- 2 pounds chicken wings

Directions:

1. In a bowl, mix the salt and pepper.
2. Add the wings to the bowl and mix with your hands to coat every last one.
3. Put 8 to 10 wings in the air fryer basket that has been sprayed with nonstick cooking spray. Set for 350 degrees F (there is no need to preheat) and cook about 15 minutes, turning once at 7 minutes.
4. Repeat with rest of wings and serve hot.

Nutrition: Calories 342 Fat 14.8 g Carbohydrates 1 g Sugar 0 g Protein 49.2 g Cholesterol 146 mg

Parmesan Chicken Wings

Preparation Time: 10 minutes

Cooking Time: 25 minutes

Serve: 4

Ingredients:

- 1 1/2 lbs. chicken wings
- 3/4 tbsp garlic powder
- 1/4 cup parmesan cheese, grated
- 2 tbsp arrowroot powder
- Salt and Pepper

Directions:

1. Preheat the air fryer to 380 F.
2. In a bowl, mix the garlic powder, parmesan cheese, arrowroot powder, pepper, and salt together. Add chicken wings and toss until well coated.
3. Put the chicken wings into the air fryer basket. Spray top of chicken wings with cooking spray.

4. Select chicken and press start. Shake air fryer basket halfway through.

5. Serve and enjoy.

Nutrition: Calories 386 Fat 15.3 g Carbohydrates 5.6 g Sugar 0.4 g Protein 53.5 g Cholesterol 160 mg

Western Chicken Wings

Preparation Time: 10 minutes

Cooking Time: 15 minutes

Serve: 4

Ingredients:

- 2 lbs. chicken wings
- 1 tsp Herb de Provence
- 1 tsp paprika
- 1/2 cup parmesan cheese, grated
- Salt and Pepper

Directions:

1. Add cheese, paprika, herb de Provence, pepper, and salt into the large mixing bowl. Place the chicken wings into the bowl and toss well to coat.
2. Preheat the air fryer to 350 F.
3. Place the chicken wings into the air fryer basket. Spray top of chicken wings with cooking spray.

4. Cook chicken wings for 15 minutes. Turn chicken wings halfway through.

5. Serve and enjoy.

Nutrition: Calories 473 Fat 19.6 g Carbohydrates 0.8 g Sugar 0.1 g Protein 69.7 g Cholesterol 211 mg

Perfect Chicken Thighs Dinner

Preparation Time: 10 minutes

Cooking Time: 15 minutes

Serve: 4

Ingredients:

- 4 chicken thighs, bone-in & skinless
- 1/4 tsp ground ginger
- 2 tsp paprika
- 2 tsp garlic powder
- salt and pepper

Directions:

1. Preheat the air fryer to 400 F.
2. In a bowl, mix ginger, paprika, garlic powder, pepper, and salt together and rub all over chicken thighs.
3. Spray chicken thighs with cooking spray.
4. Place chicken thighs into the air fryer basket and cook for 10 minutes.
5. Turn chicken thighs and cook for 5 minutes more.

6. Serve and enjoy.

Nutrition: Calories 286 Fat 11 g Carbohydrates 1.8 g Sugar 0.5 g Protein 42.7 g Cholesterol 130 mg

Perfectly Spiced Chicken Tenders

Preparation Time: 10 minutes

Cooking Time: 13 minutes

Serve: 4

Ingredients:

- 6 chicken tenders
- 1 tsp onion powder
- 1 tsp garlic powder
- 1 tsp paprika
- 1 tsp kosher salt

Directions:

1. Preheat the air fryer to 380 F.
2. In a bowl, mix onion powder, garlic powder, paprika, and salt together and rub all over chicken tenders.
3. Spray chicken tenders with cooking spray.
4. Place chicken tenders into the air fryer basket and cook for 13 minutes.
5. Serve and enjoy.

Nutrition: Calories 423 Fat 16.4 g Carbohydrates 1.5 g Sugar 0.5 g Protein 63.7 g Cholesterol 195 mg

SEAFOOD RECIPES

Air Fried Cod with Basil Vinaigrette

Preparation Time: 20 minutes

Cooking Time: 15 minutes

Servings: 4

Ingredients:

- ¼ cup olive oil
- 4 cod fillets
- A bunch of basil, torn
- Juice from 1 lemon, freshly squeezed
- Salt and pepper to taste

Directions:

1. Preheat the air fryer for 5 minutes.

2. Season the cod fillets with salt and pepper to taste.

3. Place in the air fryer and cook for 15 minutes at 3500F.

4. Meanwhile, mix the rest of the ingredients in a bowl and toss to combine.

5. Serve the air fried cod with the basil vinaigrette.

Nutrition: Calories: 235 Carbohydrates: 1.9g Protein: 14.3g Fat: 18.9g

Almond Flour Coated Crispy Shrimps

Preparation Time: 15 minutes

Cooking Time: 10 minutes

Servings: 4

Ingredients:

- ½ cup almond flour
- 1 tablespoon yellow mustard
- 1-pound raw shrimps, peeled and deveined
- 3 tablespoons olive oil
- Salt and pepper to taste

Directions:

1. Place all ingredients in a Ziploc bag and give a good shake.

2. Place in the air fryer and cook for 10 minutes at 4000F.

Nutrition: Calories: 206 Carbohydrates: 1.3g Protein: 23.5g Fat: 11.9g

Another Crispy Coconut Shrimp Recipe

Preparation Time: 20 minutes

Cooking Time: 20 minutes

Servings: 4

Ingredients:

- ½ cup flour
- ½ stick cold butter, cut into cubes
- ½ tablespoon lemon juice
- 1 egg yolk, beaten
- 1 green onion, chopped
- 1-pound salmon fillets, cut into small cubes
- 3 tablespoons whipping cream

- 4 eggs, beaten
- Salt and pepper to taste

Directions:

1. Preheat the air fryer to 3900F.
2. Season salmon fillets with lemon juice, salt and pepper.
3. In another bowl, combine the flour and butter. Add cold water gradually to form a dough. Knead the dough on a flat surface to form a sheet.
4. Place the dough on the baking dish and press firmly on the dish.
5. Beat the eggs and egg yolk and season with salt and pepper to taste.
6. Place the salmon cubes on the pan lined with dough and pour the egg over.
7. Cook for 15 to 20 minutes.
8. Garnish with green onions once cooked.

Nutrition: Calories per serving: 483 Carbs: 5.2g Protein: 45.2 Fat: 31.2g

Apple Slaw Topped Alaskan Cod Filet

Preparation Time: 10 minutes

Cooking Time: 15 minutes

Servings: 3

Ingredients:

- ¼ cup mayonnaise
- ½ red onion, diced
- 1 ½ pounds frozen Alaskan cod
- 1 box whole wheat panko bread crumbs
- 1 granny smith apple, julienned
- 1 tablespoon vegetable oil
- 1 teaspoon paprika
- 2 cups Napa cabbage, shredded

- Salt and pepper to taste

Directions:

1. Preheat the air fryer to 3900F.

2. Place the grill pan accessory in the air fryer.

3. Brush the fish with oil and dredge in the breadcrumbs.

4. Place the fish on the grill pan and cook for 15 minutes. Make sure to flip the fish halfway through the cooking time.

5. Meanwhile, prepare the slaw by mixing the remaining ingredients in a bowl.

6. Serve the fish with the slaw.

Nutrition: Calories per serving: 316 Carbs: 13.5g Protein: 37.8g Fat: 12.2g

Baked Cod Fillet Recipe From Thailand

Preparation Time: 15 minutes

Cooking Time: 20 minutes

Servings: 4

Ingredients:

- ¼ cup coconut milk, freshly squeezed
- 1 tablespoon lime juice, freshly squeezed
- 1-pound cod fillet, cut into bite-sized pieces
- Salt and pepper to taste

Directions:

1. Preheat the air fryer for 5 minutes.

2. Place all ingredients in a baking dish that will fit in the air fryer.

3. Place in the air fryer.

4. Cook for 20 minutes at 3250F.

Nutrition: Calories per serving: 844 Carbohydrates: 2.3g Protein: 21.6g Fat: 83.1g

Baked Scallops With Garlic Aioli

Preparation Time: 15 minutes

Cooking Time: 10 minutes

Servings: 4

Ingredients:

- 1 cup bread crumbs
- 1/4 cup chopped parsley
- 16 sea scallops, rinsed and drained
- 2 shallots, chopped
- 3 pinches ground nutmeg
- 4 tablespoons olive oil
- 5 cloves garlic, minced
- 5 tablespoons butter, melted
- Salt and pepper to taste

Directions:

1. Lightly grease baking pan of air fryer with cooking spray.
2. Mix in shallots, garlic, melted butter, and scallops. Season with pepper, salt, and nutmeg.
3. In a small bowl, whisk well olive oil and bread crumbs. Sprinkle over scallops.
4. For 10 minutes, cook on 390oF until tops are lightly browned.
5. Serve and enjoy with a sprinkle of parsley.

Nutrition: Calories per Serving: 452 Carbs: 29.8g Protein: 15.2g Fat: 30.2g

Basil 'N Lime-Chili Clams

Preparation Time: 10 minutes

Cooking Time: 15 minutes

Servings: 3

Ingredients:

- ½ cup basil leaves
- ½ cup tomatoes, chopped
- 1 tablespoon fresh lime juice
- 25 littleneck clams
- 4 cloves of garlic, minced
- 6 tablespoons unsalted butter
- Salt and pepper to taste

Directions:

1. Preheat the air fryer to 3900F.
2. Place the grill pan accessory in the air fryer.

3. On a large foil, place all ingredients. Fold over the foil and close by crimping the edges.

4. Place on the grill pan and cook for 15 minutes.

5. Serve with bread.

Nutrition: Calories per serving: 163 Carbs: 4.1g Protein: 1.7g Fat: 15.5g

Bass Filet In Coconut Sauce

Preparation Time: 20 minutes

Cooking Time: 15 minutes

Servings: 4

Ingredients:

- ¼ cup coconut milk
- ½ pound bass fillet
- 1 tablespoon olive oil
- 2 tablespoons jalapeno, chopped
- 2 tablespoons lime juice, freshly squeezed
- 3 tablespoons parsley, chopped
- Salt and pepper to taste

Directions:

1. Preheat the air fryer for 5 minutes

---

2. Season the bass with salt and pepper to taste

3. Brush the surface with olive oil.

4. Place in the air fryer and cook for 15 minutes at 3500F.

5. Meanwhile, place in a saucepan, the coconut milk, lime juice, jalapeno and parsley.

6. Heat over medium flame.

7. Serve the fish with the coconut sauce.

Nutrition: Calories per serving: 139 Carbohydrates: 2.7g Protein: 8.7g Fat: 10.3

Beer Battered Cod Filet

Preparation Time: 10 minutes

Cooking Time: 15 minutes

Servings: 2

Ingredients:

- ½ cup all-purpose flour

- ¾ teaspoon baking powder

- 1 ¼ cup lager beer

- 2 cod fillets

- 2 eggs, beaten

- Salt and pepper to taste

Directions:

1. Preheat the air fryer to 3900F.

2. Pat the fish fillets dry then set aside.

3. In a bowl, combine the rest of the ingredients to create a batter.

4. Dip the fillets on the batter and place on the double layer rack.

5. Cook for 15 minutes.

Nutrition: Calories per serving: 229 Carbs: 33.2g Protein: 31.1g Fat: 10.2g

Buttered Baked Cod with Wine

Preparation Time: 15 minutes

Cooking Time: 12 minutes

Servings: 2

Ingredients:

- 1 tablespoon butter
- 1 tablespoon butter
- 2 tablespoons dry white wine
- 1/2 pound thick-cut cod loin
- 1-1/2 teaspoons chopped fresh parsley
- 1-1/2 teaspoons chopped green onion
- 1/2 lemon, cut into wedges
- 1/4 sleeve buttery round crackers (such as Ritz®), crushed

- 1/4 lemon, juiced

Directions:

1. In a small bowl, melt butter in microwave. Whisk in crackers.

2. Lightly grease baking pan of air fryer with remaining butter. And melt for 2 minutes at 390oF.

3. In a small bowl whisk well lemon juice, white wine, parsley, and green onion.

4. Coat cod filets in melted butter. Pour dressing. Top with butter-cracker mixture.

5. Cook for 10 minutes at 390oF.

6. Serve and enjoy with a slice of lemon.

Nutrition: Calories per Serving: 266 Carbs: 9.3g Protein: 20.9g Fat: 16.1g

Buttered Garlic-Oregano On Clams

Preparation Time: 10 minutes

Cooking Time: 5 minutes

Servings: 4

Ingredients:

- ¼ cup parmesan cheese, grated
- ¼ cup parsley, chopped
- 1 cup breadcrumbs
- 1 teaspoon dried oregano
- 2 dozen clams, shucked
- 3 cloves of garlic, minced
- 4 tablespoons butter, melted

Directions:

1. In a medium bowl, mix together the breadcrumbs, parmesan cheese, parsley, oregano, and garlic. Stir in the melted butter.
2. Preheat the air fryer to 3900F.
3. Place the baking dish accessory in the air fryer and place the clams.
4. Sprinkle the crumb mixture over the clams.
5. Cook for 5 minutes.

Nutrition: Calories per serving: 160 Carbs: 6.3g Protein: 2.9g Fat: 13.6g

Butterflied Prawns with Garlic-Sriracha

Preparation Time: 10 minutes

Cooking Time: 15 minutes

Servings: 2

Ingredients:

- 1 tablespoon lime juice
- 1 tablespoon sriracha
- 1-pound large prawns, shells removed and cut lengthwise or butterflied
- 1teaspoon fish sauce
- 2 tablespoons melted butter
- 2 tablespoons minced garlic
- Salt and pepper to taste

Directions:

1. Preheat the air fryer to 3900F.
2. Place the grill pan accessory in the air fryer.
3. Season the prawns with the rest of the ingredients.

4. Place on the grill pan and cook for 15 minutes. Make sure to flip the prawns halfway through the cooking time.

Nutrition: Calories per serving: 443 Carbs: 9.7 g Protein: 62.8g Fat: 16.9g

Cajun Seasoned Salmon Filet

Preparation Time: 10 minutes

Cooking Time: 15 minutes

Servings: 1

Ingredients:

- 1 salmon fillet
- 1 teaspoon juice from lemon, freshly squeezed
- 3 tablespoons extra virgin olive oil
- A dash of Cajun seasoning mix
- Salt and pepper to taste

Directions:

1. Preheat the air fryer for 5 minutes.
2. Place all ingredients in a bowl and toss to coat.
3. Place the fish fillet in the air fryer basket.
4. Bake for 15 minutes at 3250F.
5. Once cooked drizzle with olive oil

Nutrition: Calories per serving: 523 Carbohydrates: 4.6g Protein: 47.9g Fat: 34.8g

Cajun Spiced Lemon-Shrimp Kebabs

Preparation Time: 15 minutes

Cooking Time: 10 minutes

Servings: 2

Ingredients:

- 1 tsp cayenne
- 1 tsp garlic powder
- 1 tsp kosher salt
- 1 tsp onion powder
- 1 tsp oregano
- 1 tsp paprika
- 12 pcs XL shrimp
- 2 lemons, sliced thinly crosswise
- 2 tbsp olive oil

Directions:

1. In a bowl, mix all ingredients except for sliced lemons. Marinate for 10 minutes.
2. Thread 3 shrimps per steel skewer.
3. Place in skewer rack.

4. Cook for 5 minutes at 390oF.

5. Serve and enjoy with freshly squeezed lemon.

Nutrition: Calories per Serving: 232 Carbs: 7.9g Protein: 15.9g Fat: 15.1g

Cajun Spiced Veggie-Shrimp Bake

Preparation Time: 15 minutes

Cooking Time: 20 minutes

Servings: 4

Ingredients:

- 1 Bag of Frozen Mixed Vegetables
- 1 Tbsp Gluten Free Cajun Seasoning
- Olive Oil Spray
- Season with salt and pepper
- Small Shrimp Peeled & Deveined (Regular Size Bag about 50-80 Small Shrimp)

Directions:

1. Lightly grease baking pan of air fryer with cooking spray. Add all ingredients and toss well to coat. Season with pepper and salt, generously.
2. For 10 minutes, cook on 330oF. Halfway through cooking time, stir.
3. Cook for 10 minutes at 330oF.
4. Serve and enjoy.

Nutrition: Calories per Serving: 78 Carbs: 13.2g

Protein: 2.8g Fat: 1.5g

Tempura Shrimp

Preparation Time: 15 minutes

Cooking Time: 10 minutes

Servings: 4

Ingredients:

- 1 package frozen shrimp tempura

Directions:

1. Spread shrimp tempura on the air fryer basket or tray; don't let them overlap to allow even cooking
2. Put them in air fryer and air fry at 380f for 10 minutes, check and flip halfway through cooking
3. Serve and enjoy

Nutrition: Calories: 21 kcal Protein: 1.6 g Fat: 1.52 g Carbohydrates: 0 g

CONCLUSION

Air fryers are a relatively new piece of kitchen gadgetry. They are used by individuals who want to cook healthy foods using less oil and less fat then their conventional counterparts.

In addition to being a healthier alternative to deep frying, air fryers are also fun to use. Air-frying not only produces lots of fun and tasty food, it also saves you time and money. You can cook without the need of a griddle or a stovetop, which frees up your kitchen so you can focus on eating more healthy foods!

It is important to have an air fryer that is up to par. If you want an air fryer that will last for years, make sure that you buy an durable one. To help you choose the right air fryer for you, we have compiled a list of the best air fried ovens!

The Airfryer has several seating options. The four different versions include:

Small Seating–The size of the seating area is 13.5" x 8.5" x 9.5".

Medium Seating–The size of the seating area is 20" x 12".

Large Seating–The size of the seating area is 23" x 15".

Extra Large Seating–The size is 32" X 21". The extra large seat could accommodate up to 8 pieces. A small, medium or large fryer is included with every air fryer and can be purchased separately. The only part that may need to be purchased separately is a colander for the basket which will hold up to 16 cups depending on the size of the basket that you are using. There are no other accessories required for the air fryer: please see the specifications on this page for further details.

What's happening to our restaurant food? The answer is rather simple. We are over-cooking and over-frying foods, and most of it is for the wrong reasons.

Nobody wants to eat overcooked, undercooked, or under-salted food. Restaurant owners are turning away good customers in the name of profit.

That's not our fault. It's up to the professional chefs to do a better job with their cooking skills.

We use our Air Fryers to cook foods that don't require cooking at all. We use them to cook and heat our foods in such a way that they're ready to eat right out of the air fryer. There's no need for you to heat up your kitchen with a conventional oven or stove, just put the food in and let it finish fully. You'll be amazed at how delicious your foods can taste when you use an Air Fryer!

Today's busy lifestyle often leaves us with little time to cook. For those of you who don't have time to cook, but still need your food, the air fryer is for you.

An air fryer is an appliance that cooks food by circulating hot air over it. The circulating air causes the food to slowly cook within a sealed container while removing excess oil and fat from the food. By sealing the food in a hermetic chamber during cooking, no additional oil is released into the air. This is important because it prevents the flavor of the food from being compromised. The result is a fast and easy way to prepare delicious meals without having to use any grease or oils while eroding your pantry of oils.

In this air fryer cookbook, we will teach you how to use your air fryer most effectively and how to avoid common mistakes. From learning how to clean and maintain your air fryer to finding creative recipes, this guide will help you get the most out of your air fryer today

CPSIA information can be obtained
at www.ICGtesting.com
Printed in the USA
LVHW080137060521
686585LV00002B/214

9 781801 838306